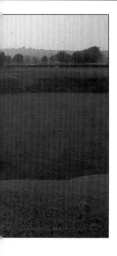

Caerleon lies 3 miles (4.8km) north-east of Newport. The B4596 leads directly from Junction 25 on the M4 into the centre of the town. There are regular bus services from Newport. Car-parks are situated at the Fortress Baths and amphitheatre sites.

Contents

D1249277

Designed by **Tom Morgan**

Edited by **David M. Robinson** *BSc, PhD, FSA*

First Published 1988

© *Cadw: Welsh Historic Monuments*
Brunel House, 2 Fitzalan Road, CARDIFF, CF2 1UY.

Typeset by Afal, Cardiff.

Printed in Great Britain by C.B.L. Ltd.

ISBN 0 948329 16 5

Roman Isca

In Search of Isca

The traveller who comes to modern Caerleon, Arthur Machen's 'noble, fallen Caerleon on Usk', in search of the Roman legionary fortress of *Isca*, will find a small town of some seven thousand people, standing beside a crossing of the tidal River Usk, and not yet wholly swallowed up by the urban sprawl of nearby Newport. The early nineteenth-century stone bridge is the successor of Roman and medieval bridges, which stood on the opposite side of the *Hanbury Arms Hotel* to the present bridge. The last of these, of timber, largely collapsed in a memorable storm in 1772 and was, after being patched up, eventually replaced. These older bridges stood on the line

where the *via praetoria*, one of the main roads of the fortress, led down to the river. In medieval and later times, merchant ships sailed from quays on the riverside here to Bristol, to Ireland and to Atlantic ports like La Rochelle or Lisbon. For the Romans, a major reason for establishing their strategic base for the conquest of south Wales here in A.D. 74 or 75, instead of the site of their existing legionary fortress at Usk, eight miles (13km) up river, would have been the ease with

A Roman legionary soldier: The illustration is based upon a reconstruction of the armour and equipment of the latter first century A.D. (Illustration by Geraint Derbyshire).

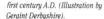

which an army on campaign could be supplied with food and munitions by sea through a base near the mouth of the Usk. The fortress itself, *Isca*, bore the name of the river.

The Roman ruins at Caerleon have attracted travellers for at least eight hundred years. In 1188 Gerald of Wales (Giraldus Cambrensis), on a recruiting tour for the Crusades, described them in phrases, which, though largely stock journalistic clichés of the day, leave no doubt that there were still imposing ruins to be seen. In 1405, a French expeditionary force in support of Owain Glyndŵr took time off to inspect the Roman amphitheatre, by then 'King Arthur's

The legionary fortress of Isca, *with its characteristic playing-card shape, seen from the air. The line of the Roman and medieval bridges is shown to the right of the present river crossing.*

Round Table'. In the reign of Elizabeth I, the topographer-poet, Thomas Churchyard, told how:

In Arthurs tyme, a table round,
Was there whereat he sate:
As yet a plot of goodly ground,
Sets foorth that rare estate...

There are such vautes and hollow caves,
Such walles and condits deepe:
Made all like pypes of earthen pots,
Wherein a child may creepe.

Such streates and pavements sondrie waies,
To every market towne...

The Worthines of Wales (London 1776), pp. 23-4,
Reprinted from the edition of 1587.

But by this time the impressive ruins seen by earlier visitors had vanished — robbed ('mooted up' was the local term) to build the houses of Caerleon. The one surviving tower of Caerleon Castle, next to the *Hanbury Arms*, is built almost entirely of Roman stones, as are almost all the older buildings in the town.

Roman finds from Caerleon: Tiles with the stamp of the Second Augustan Legion, coins, a lamp, and a fragment of a Trajanic building inscription (From E. Donovan, Descriptive Excursions through South Wales and Monmouthshire, *London 1805*).

The surviving thirteenth-century tower of Caerleon Castle, next to the Hanbury Arms, is built of reused stone robbed from Roman buildings.

By the late eighteenth century, travellers and scholars were recording Roman finds dug up at Caerleon. These included coins, fragments of inscriptions and sculpture, together with tiles marked with the legionary stamp, LEG II AUG, which confirmed that this was indeed the base of the Second Augustan Legion. Most of these relics were sold to visitors or were lost, and Roman inscriptions were reused as building material or broken up to mend the roads. Eventually, John Edward Lee, a Yorkshireman who had settled in Caerleon when he became a partner in a Newport nail factory, persuaded the gentry of the county to join him in building a museum to preserve such finds. The museum was opened in 1850, and Lee himself was also instrumental in the foundation of the Caerleon (now the Monmouthshire) Antiquarian Association. In time, however, the upkeep of the museum proved too much for a local society, and in 1931 the National Museum of Wales took over responsibility.

The old town of Caerleon occupied only a small part of the area of the Roman fortress, much of which was still open fields, but by the early part of this century the town was growing, and previously untouched parts of the buried remains were beginning to disappear under modern housing. A start was made on the archaeological exploration of the fortress in 1908, when land which was to be used to extend the churchyard was excavated. Systematic rescue work, whereby plans of parts of the fortress were recovered before they were destroyed by building developments, began in 1926 when a local excavation committee was set up on the initiative of the director of the National Museum of Wales, Mortimer Wheeler. It was Wheeler who also persuaded the *Daily Mail* to sponsor the excavation of the Roman amphitheatre ('King Arthur's Round Table'), and to present the excavated remains to the then Office of Works (the predecessors of Cadw: Welsh Historic Monuments) as a national monument.

Wheeler persuaded the Daily Mail to sponsor the excavation of the amphitheatre, and the newspaper carried regular reports.

HISTORIC SITE
FOR
THE NATION.

BRITAIN'S BIGGEST ROMAN AMPHITHEATRE.

GIFT BY "THE DAILY MAIL."

EXCAVATIONS TO BE BEGUN.

We are able to announce to-day the conclusion of negotiations by which one of the most interesting Roman sites in Britain will be preserved, excavated, and handed over to the nation.

The site—at Caerleon, in Monmouthshire—is that of the largest Roman amphitheatre in the kingdom where in the days of the Caesars gladiators fought and, according to tradition, Christian martyrs were put to death as they were in the great Colosseum in Rome.

WHERE GLADIATORS FOUGHT.

Right: Dr [Sir] R. E. Mortimer Wheeler, at about the time of his excavation of the amphitheatre at Caerleon, 1926-27 (By permission of the National Museum of Wales).

Below: The 1926-27 excavations on the amphitheatre in progress (By permission of the National Museum of Wales).

When a large field in the western angle of the fortress, known as Prysg Field, came on the market as building land in 1927, the local committee raised £2,500 to buy it and a member of the staff at the National Museum, Victor Nash-Williams, excavated it. His work revealed a row of Roman barracks, which were also given to the Office of Works. In the subsequent sixty years there has been an archaeological 'rescue' excavation at Caerleon almost every year, save during the Second World War, often in advance of housing development. An almost complete outline plan of the fortress has been recovered in this way, and parts — the amphitheatre, Prysg Field barracks, Fortress Baths and the south-western defences — are now on view to the public; and many of the finds from Isca are displayed by the National Museum of Wales in the Legionary Museum. Almost all significant pieces of undeveloped ground within the fortress and its suburbs are now protected as Scheduled Ancient Monuments.

Dr V. E. Nash-Williams of the National Museum of Wales, director of many excavations at Caerleon. He is seen here at work on the civil settlement to the south-west of the fortress (By permission of the National Museum of Wales).

The legionary barracks in the Prysg Field (see pp. 41-6), excavated by V. E. Nash-Williams.

The Legion and its Fortress

In the second century of the Christian era, the empire of Rome comprehended the fairest part of the earth, and the most civilized portion of mankind. The frontiers of that extensive monarchy were guarded by ancient renown and disciplined valour.

Edward Gibbon
The History of the Decline and Fall of the Roman Empire,
3 vols (London 1776-81), chapter 1.

The Second Augustan Legion (*Legio Secunda Augusta*) was one of about thirty Roman legions whose fortresses guarded the frontiers of the empire from Inchtuthil on the edge of the Scottish Highlands to Bostra in the Arabian desert. Each legion was a division of about 5,500 heavy armed infantry, all Roman citizens, with all the necessary support services included. *Legio II Augusta* was named after the emperor Augustus, who had raised it, much as a modern regiment might be called the King's Own, or the Queen's Regiment. Legions usually had both a number and a title, the latter sometimes a nickname in

The Capricorn insignia of the Second Augustan Legion, the birth sign of its founder, the Emperor Augustus. From a silver denarius of the Emperor Vespasian (By permission of the National Museum of Wales).

Roman Legionary Fortresses

Not all the fortresses were occupied at the same time. The map also shows the previous fortresses of the legions which came to Britain.

☐ *Extent of the Roman Empire*

1. Inchtuthil	9. Gloucester
2. Carpow	10. Colchester
3. York	11. Exeter
4. Chester	12. Neuss
5. Wroxeter	13. Mainz
6. Lincoln	14. Strasbourg
7. Caerleon	15. Siscia
8. Usk	

0   1000KM

origin (*VI Ferrata*, 'The Ironsides' or 'Iron Shod'); sometimes the name of a province in which they had served with distinction (*IX Hispana*, 'Spanish'); or sometimes a battle honour (*XX Valeria Victrix*, granted the extra title 'Victorious'

The Emperor Augustus, from a coin – a silver denarius *(By permission of the National Museum of Wales).*

following their rôle in the defeat of Boudica [Boadicea]). From time to time a legion would be destroyed in battle or perhaps disbanded after a mutiny or a failed coup, and new legions would sometimes be raised. Hence, the legionary numbers were not a consecutive series and there were other second legions besides *II Augusta*.

The commanding officer was a legionary legate, from an aristocratic family of senatorial rank, who held command as part of a career structure as senior soldier and administrator. He had served his military apprenticeship as senior tribune or staff officer in a legion and, if he measured up to the job, he might look forward to being appointed by the emperor to a provincial governorship, and perhaps to the dignity of the consulship in Rome. Below him there were six tribunes, the senior being a young man of similar background to the legate, but the others were from more modest families ('Roman knights'). They also followed career paths as soldiers and administrators, though in lower grade posts than those reserved for the senatorial aristocracy.

The sixty centuries, of eighty men each, into which the legion was divided were commanded by centurions. Usually promoted from the ranks, these formidable figures were the backbone of the legion. Whilst it might not be too misleading to invest the centurion with some of the popular attributes of the modern Sergeant Major (and some of Kipling's unflattering portraits of late Victorian Sergeant Majors in India would probably

have been instantly recognizable to a ranker of *Legio II Augusta*) his responsibilities were more equivalent to those of the modern company commander — a major or a senior captain — with full charge of his eighty men.

The Foundation of Isca

Legio II Augusta was stationed at Strasbourg on the Rhine frontier when it was chosen by the emperor Claudius to take part in the invasion of Britain in A.D. 43. It served with distinction under its commander Titus Flavius Vespasianus, under whom it reduced an impressive number of hillforts in south-west England. Vespasian, by then commanding the Roman army against the

The ramparts of the great hillfort of Maiden Castle, Dorset, seen from the air. It was stormed by the Second Legion under the future Emperor Vespasian. A battle cemetery of the legion's victims has been found in excavation (By courtesy of English Heritage).

Jews in Palestine, made a bid for the imperial throne during the civil war which followed the suicide of Nero in A.D. 69; and *II Augusta* played a central rôle in persuading the other British legions to declare for its old commanding officer. Vespasian was to become the first emperor of the new Flavian dynasty.

Judea Capta — *A coin of Vespasian, proclaiming his conquest of the Jews (By permission of the National Museum of Wales).*

At this time, *Legio II Augusta* was still in southwest England, stationed at another *Isca*, the later Exeter. Excavations in recent years have revealed

parts of the fortress there, including a bath building which must have been as large as the Caerleon Fortress Baths (pp. 18-30), together with a rank of timber barrack blocks. The new emperor, who had made his reputation as a fighting soldier on the frontiers of the empire in Judaea and Britain, began a new forward policy in the as yet unconquered areas of Britain. The governor of an active military province like Britain would be chosen by the emperor with special regard to the task in hand, and to his particular experience and ability. Vespasian's first governor, Petillius Cerialis (A.D. 71-4), had the task of settling affairs in northern England, but once this had been done, the next priority was the final pacification of what is now Wales.

Vespasian's choice for this task was Sextus Julius Frontinus (governor A.D. 74-8), an experienced soldier and in later life the writer of important books on military tactics and on the water supply of Rome (he became director of the city's water supply and aqueducts). The historian Tacitus, whose praise was not easily won, thought him 'a truly great man . . . he conquered the powerful and warlike tribe of the Silures, overcoming not only a fierce and stubborn enemy, but the difficulties of the terrain'.

The hillfort of Caerau, near Llantrisant, seen from the air. It was possibly the seat of a Silurian chieftain (By courtesy of the Glamorgan-Gwent Archaelogical Trust).

The Silures, whose territories included the modern counties of Brecknock, the Glamorgans and Gwent, had resisted a series of Roman governors for nearly thirty years, and had inflicted several severe reverses on the legions. Frontinus's strategy was to move the Second Legion to a new fortress well inside Silurian territory, but on a site where the supplies for a large army could be brought in by sea. Cerialis had done much the same thing a few years earlier in the north, and the soundness of his choice for *Legio IX*'s new fortress is endorsed by the later history of the city of York.

Roman Forts

• Legionary Fortress   • Fortlet
▨ Legionary Fortress evacuated   — Roads
• Auxiliary Fort

The site chosen by Frontinus was an area of flat unencumbered land at a good bridging point of the Usk, and close enough to its mouth to be reached easily by sea-going ships. The new fortress was protected by a broad loop of the river and by a small tributary, the Afon Lwyd, but was on gently elevated ground clear of the floodplain with a suitable gradient for drains and sewers. No traces of an earlier fort have been found on the site, despite many years of excavation, though one might be expected somewhere in the vicinity, for the Romans had occupied much of south-east Wales by the mid 50s. However, until the river was bridged, and docking facilities built, the site of the later fortress would have had no overriding advantage. A small, Roman fort, earlier than the existing fortress, may remain undiscovered somewhere in the Caerleon area, but it will have been sited for tactical rather than for strategic reasons.

The Layout of the Fortress

The fortress covered an area of some 50 acres (20.5ha), shaped rather like a playing-card. The angles of the great sweeping defences were rounded for greater stability and a better field of fire. There were four gates, one in the centre of each side, though nothing of these now remains above ground.

The Defences

When first built, about A.D. 75, the defences were of turf, clay and timber. Only later, about A.D. 100-10, was the bank fronted with a wall of mortared masonry, and its timber gates and towers replaced in stone.

Legionaries were skilled in the art of building turf and clay ramparts. Sometimes a foundation of oak logs was laid under the bank to provide a firm foundation. Indeed, strapping of this kind was found under part of the rampart in Prysg Field, though only, it seems, in one small area. Turves

An artist's impression of soldiers building defences of turf and clay, digging the fort ditch with picks and removing soil in baskets. Turves were cut to regulation size, capable of being carried by one man, and carefully built up in layers (Illustration by Peter Connolly).

The Prysg Field barracks as they might have appeared in the late first century. The defences and barracks are of timber, the rampart (seen in section) is of layered clay and turf (Illustration by John Banbury after Howard Mason).

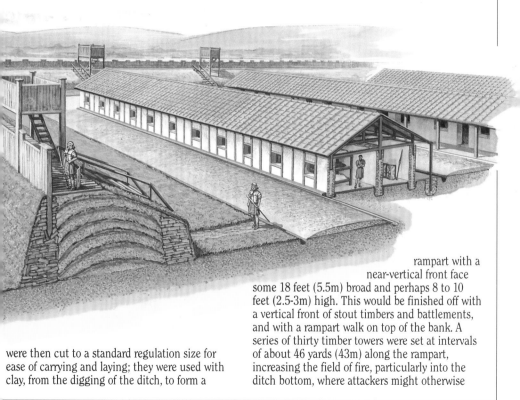

were then cut to a standard regulation size for ease of carrying and laying; they were used with clay, from the digging of the ditch, to form a rampart with a near-vertical front face some 18 feet (5.5m) broad and perhaps 8 to 10 feet (2.5-3m) high. This would be finished off with a vertical front of stout timbers and battlements, and with a rampart walk on top of the bank. A series of thirty timber towers were set at intervals of about 46 yards (43m) along the rampart, increasing the field of fire, particularly into the ditch bottom, where attackers might otherwise shelter out of reach of missiles from the rampart. The towers may also have mounted spring guns or heavy crossbows, with which the legion was well provided. Inside the bank a perimeter road, the *via sagularis*, gave troops rapid access to the rampart in case of attack.

In front of the bank was the fortress ditch, now entirely silted up, though cross-sections have been cut archaeologically at a number of points. The ditch was around 8 or 9 feet (2.5 or 2.7m) deep and about 26 feet (8m) wide. The profile was 'V'-shaped where it cut through the clay, but was flatter where it met the sandstone bedrock. With its sloping sides of slippery clay, and its bottom silted with wet, black mud, it would have presented a formidable obstacle.

The Internal Layout

Within the defences, the buildings were laid out to a pattern standard in legionary fortresses. With rare exceptions — notably the Fortress Baths — they were first constructed of timber. Before modern techniques of 'open area' excavation were in use, archaeologists usually concentrated on the later stone buildings, exploring the earlier timber phase only in narrow cuttings. Thus, our knowledge of the first-century fortress is very limited, though where it has been tested, its basic layout is largely followed in the later stone-built arrangement.

For an account of the buildings within the fortress, other than those on public view, the reader is referred to the publications by Mr G. C. Boon of the National Museum of Wales (see Further Reading p. 47). Here, only the barest detail is given, to show what buildings were necessary for the legion.

In the centre of the fortress (in the area under the present church) was the *principia* or headquarters, where the legionary eagle and standards were kept and a statue of the reigning emperor displayed. Across the *via principalis*, the street in front of the headquarters, was a row of officers' houses. Behind the *principia* was the official residence of the legionary legate. The *via principalis* itself divided the fortress into two equal halves. The front half (*praetentura*) held the Fortress Baths and the hospital. The rear (*retentura*) contained the workshops for the legionary craftsmen — including masons,

carpenters, blacksmiths, tanners, shoemakers (5,500 pairs of military boots would have needed constant repair) and others. Unexcavated areas within the defences would have held the granaries, together with a range of other buildings including a prison.

'Imperial Caesar, son of Divine Nerva, Nerva Trajan Augustus, conqueror of Germany . . .' An inscription on Tuscan marble recording the rebuilding of one of the major buildings or gates of the fortress in stone in A.D. 100 (By permission of the National Museum of Wales).

The Layout of the Fortress

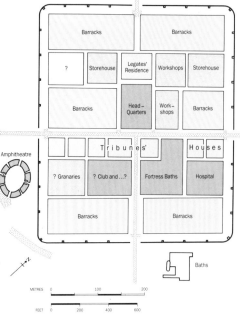

The front and rear ranges of the fortress and areas flanking the *principia* held the ranges of long narrow barrack-blocks, one for each century, six for each of the ten cohorts, and therefore sixty in all (though at the time Caerleon was founded the first cohort of each legion comprised five double centuries and therefore needed additional barracks). This layout was repeated, with some variation, at fortresses throughout the empire, and legionaries newly posted to *II Augusta* from north Africa or the Danube would have found their way around *Isca* without undue difficulty.

An antefix, or decorative roof finial, showing Cupid between a pair of dolphins (By permission of the National Museum of Wales).

The basilica *or recreation hall of the Fortress Baths. The naves of the first Christian churches derived from architecturally similar basilicas found in Roman palaces and other buildings (After Zienkiewicz 1986).*

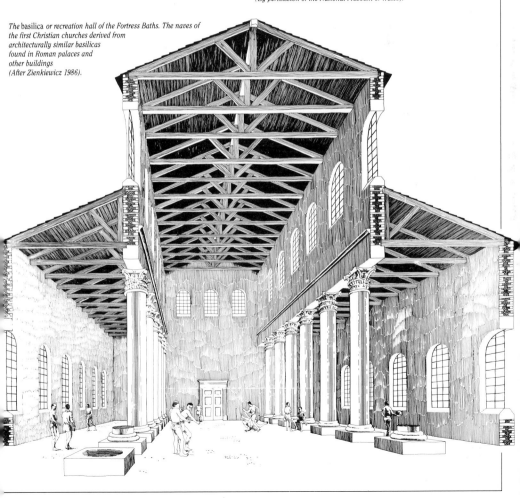

The Second Legion and the Occupation of Caerleon

The legion contained over 5,000 men but, save in the initial campaign against the Silures, the whole force would rarely have fought together as a single unit. Detachments or vexillations, so known from their *vexillum* or banner, were detached for campaigns in northern Britain or on one of the other frontiers of the empire. There are numerous records of such vexillations of *II Augusta* and a tombstone from Caerleon was set up by a lady to her mother and to her brother, Tadius Exupertus, who died 'on the German campaign'. With Siluria peaceful, an

Hadrian ordered a wall to be built from the Tyne to the Solway, to separate the people of the Roman province from the unconquered area to the north. This section is near the fort of Housesteads (By courtesy of English Heritage).

The Emperor Hadrian (A.D. 117-38), from a coin (By permission of the National Museum of Wales).

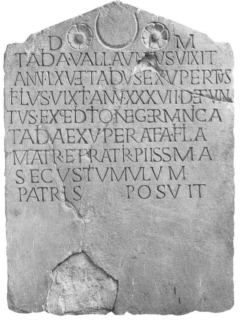

'To the Gods of the Underworld. Tadia Vallaunius lived 65 years. Her son Tadius Exsuperatus lived 37 years and died on the German campaign . . .' A tombstone from Caerleon, now in the Legionary Museum (By permission of the National Museum of Wales).

much of the Roman army in Britain was drafted to this area. Inscriptions from Hadrian's Wall record the efforts of the many craftsmen, including stonemasons, from seven out of ten cohorts of *II Augusta* who were at work there. The absence of

An inscription from milecastle 38 (Hotbanks) on the central sector of Hadrian's Wall, recording Legio II Augusta at work there under the governor Aulus Platorius Nepos (last line) in A.D. 122-26.

increasing number of troops could be drafted away. Barracks would be left empty and *Isca* became, increasingly, a regimental base depot rather than an active military garrison.

When the emperor Hadrian began his great frontier wall across northern Britain in A.D. 122,

the other three from the surviving inscriptions may be due to chance. When the Roman frontier was advanced into southern Scotland under Antoninus Pius twenty years later, a fresh series of inscriptions show that much of the legion was still on the northern frontier.

It was once thought that with the legion away, *Isca* lay empty at this time, but archaeological evidence shows that occupation continued, at least in some parts of the fortress. Our evidence is too slight to reconstruct what must have been complicated troop movements, but at the Prysg Field barracks it would seem that only some of them were occupied, perhaps one per cohort. It may have been that each cohort needed to maintain a presence at the base depot for recruits, soldiers rejoining their unit or waiting to be reassigned. Indeed, base depots can be busy places in wartime, even if the unit is on active service elsewhere.

The murder of the emperor Commodus in A.D. 192 ended the Antonine age — the 'high summer' of the empire. In the ensuing scramble for power, Septimius Severus eventually emerged as the victor. In the process, he had bloodily defeated at Lyon British legions, including *II Augusta*, who had supported the British contender for power, Clodius Albinus. The withdrawal of the army from Britain opened the gates to Caledonian invaders, and the northern frontier was overrun. It took a series of hard fought campaigns in the north and in Scotland, some led by the emperor in person, before stability was restored.

A fine inscription dug up in the churchyard at Caerleon records the restoration of the headquarters building under Severus and his sons Caracalla and Geta sometime before the latter was murdered by his brother in 211. On this, and on one of the two inscriptions set up by a legionary prefect for the health and safety of the imperial family, Geta's name ahs been erased by order of his brother — he had become what George Orwell might call an 'unperson'.

The church of St Cadoc stands on the site of the headquarters building of Isca. The inscription is from the churchyard, and records that the headquarters, which had fallen into decay (corruptum), was restored by the Emperor Septimius Severus (A.D. 197-211 — right) and his sons Caracalla and Geta. The latter's name was partly erased after his murder. Only part of the inscription has been found.

IMPERATORES	CAESARES·L·SEPTI	MIVS SEVERVS PIVS	PERTINAX AVG·ET	· M · AVRELIVS
ANTONINVS A	VG·ET·P·SEPTIMIVS	GETA NOBILISSIMVS	CAESAR	
VETVSTATE C	ORRVPTVM ∅			RESTITVERVNT ∅

The legionary headquarters was evidently here in the early part of Severus's reign, when the northern frontier was gradually being restored. At this time, *II Augusta* was no doubt being brought back to full strength after its heavy losses at Lyon and the subsequent very thorough purge of officers loyal to Clodius Albinus. By 208 Severus was ready to take the offensive in Scotland and *II Augusta* would have marched north. During these campaign years, part of the legion was stationed in a new legionary base at Carpow on the Tay. Caracalla made peace in 211-12 and soon after this the *Isca* fortress was extensively renovated. The south-west gate, near the amphitheatre, may have been restored under Caracalla, judging by an inscription found near it. In addition, the amphitheatre was remodelled and barrack-blocks were repaired and rerooved. The legionary tile kilns were busy producing large quantities of roofing tiles, stamped LEG II AVG ANT, with the title *Antoniniana* — 'Caracalla's Own' — granted to the legion by the emperor. About 214-17, during a period at *Isca*, the legionary legate Tiberius

Claudius Paulinus may have become patron of the town of *Venta Silurum* (Caerwent). Later in his career he was able to obtain some substantial official favour for the town, and was honoured by the grateful local authority with a statue.

The base of the statue of Tiberius Claudius Paulinus, former commanding officer of the Second Augustan Legion, from Caerwent. It now stands in the church porch there.

The present village of Caerwent stands within the massive defences of the Roman town of Venta Silurum.

Severus died at York in A.D. 211. He was followed by the new Emperor Caracalla, seen here on a coin — antoninianus (By permission of the National Museum of Wales).

Caracalla granted the Second Legion the title Antoniniana ('Caracalla's Own'), which appears on tiles from Caerleon — evidence that considerable building works were taking place in and around the fortress at this time. (By permission of the National Museum of Wales).

The campaigns of Severus maintained stability in Britain for two generations, and the army went about the routine business of peace-time soldiering. At Caerleon, the Fortress Baths were maintained down to 230 or 240 and some of the Prysg Field barracks were seemingly occupied until the same date. In 234, and again in 244, we have evidence that the *primus pilus* or senior centurion of *Legio II Augusta* dedicated an altar to the Eagle of the legion on its official birthday (23 September) at a ceremonial parade attended by the units of the legion then at

Caerleon. However, the murders of the emperors Severus Alexander in 235 and of Gordian III in 244 began a period of political, and economic anarchy, and by the time the next such ceremony was due, the core of the legion may have been called away to fight for one of the numerous and ephemeral emperors of the third century.

This was not the end of *Isca*. Most of it lay empty and the Fortress Baths and perhaps other main buildings seem to have been in the hands of a care and maintenance squad. It may well have been that the number of soldiers still there did not justify such extensive facilities and one of the smaller extra-mural baths could have sufficed. None the less, it was still the legionary base depot, and in 253-8 the seventh cohort was posted back there after a spell on duty elsewhere. Their barracks needed to be totally rebuilt. A recently discovered inscription records further building activity under Aurelian in 274-5 — perhaps more barracks.

A coin of the usurper Carausius (A.D. 286-96). The fortress of Isca may have been finally given up by the Roman army in his time, when the legion was needed to guard the south coasts against invasion from legitimate emperors (By permission of the National Museum of Wales).

The end seems to have come for *Isca* when the usurper Carausius, who had seized power in Britain, expected invasion by the legitimate emperors from the Continent. Sometime between 287 and 296 he, or his murderer and successor Allectus, may have demolished the main buildings of the fortress, possibly so that the materials could be shipped to the coast for reuse in new defences along the south-east shore of Britain. At Caerleon, a scatter of early fourth-century coins suggests that occupation of some kind continued for a while, but it is doubtful whether this was military. There were indeed fourth-century military defences along the south Wales coastal plain, notably at Caerwent and Cardiff, but Caerleon itself seems to have been ignored. The courtyard of the baths *basilica* was used as a cattle pen, and low-quality dwellings or stalls were put up in parts of the former surrounding portico. The bare shell of the Fortress Baths was to survive through to medieval times, but by this time the history of *Isca* was long over and that of Caerleon had begun.

Fourth-century silvered bronze fitting, perhaps from a bowl or dish, showing vexillations (detatchments) of two British legions – II Augusta and XX Valeria Victrix – brigaded together. The owner, Aurelius Cervianus, is urged to 'use this and be happy'. The find spot is unknown (By courtesy of the Bibliotheque Nationale, Paris).

The walls of the late-Roman fort at Cardiff, perhaps built to protect the Bristol Channel area from Irish raiders.

Roman Isca – A Tour Guide

The Roman monuments of Caerleon are all within a few minutes walk, in and around the very pleasant small town. Visitors arriving at the Fortress Baths in the centre of the town may then walk some eighty yards (73m) down the main street to the Legionary Museum by the church. From the museum, a quiet road (locally known as Broadway), on the line of the roman *via principalis* leads down to the amphitheatre. barracks and fortress wall.

The Fortress Baths

At the end of the car-park, under a handsome modern cover-building, are parts of the legionary Fortress Baths, so named to distinguish them from other bath buildings outside the fortress defences. Standing in the car-park, the visitor may care to pause and put the building into its setting. At this point, High Street is on the line of the *via praetoria*, one of the main roads of the fortress, which led up from the bridge across the Usk to the headquarters building in the centre. In Roman times, the area of the car-park would have been a large colonnaded courtyard (*palaestra*) for open-air games and exercise. At its far end, under the front of the cover-building, was a long narrow open-air swimming pool or *natatio*, with an apsidal fountain house at one (the left) end. Behind this was the bath building proper, comprising a succession of three lofty, domed halls. On the left, within the cover-building, the first of these halls was the cold bath suite or *frigidarium*. This led on to the right (under the modern gardens and houses) to the warm bath suite or *tepidarium* and the hot baths or *caldarium*. To the left of the cover-building (below

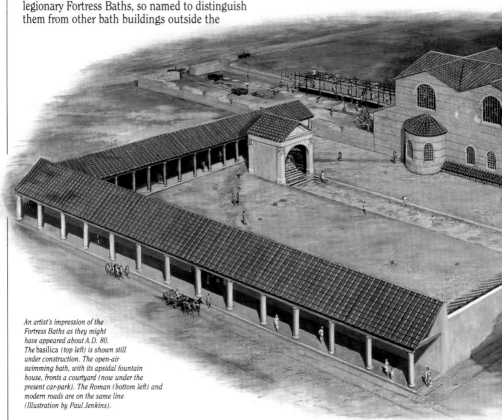

An artist's impression of the Fortress Baths as they might have appeared about A.D. 80. The basilica (top left) is shown still under construction. The open-air swimming bath, with its apsidal fountain house, fronts a courtyard (now under the present car-park). The Roman (bottom left) and modern roads are on the same line (Illustration by Paul Jenkins).

more modern gardens and houses) was an aisled hall or *basilica*, which in plan and scale matched the nave of a medieval cathedral (see illustration p. 13)

Our knowledge concerning the overall plan and development of the baths as a whole is based upon a series of detailed archaeological excavations extending over a number of years. The site was discovered and explored between 1964-81. On entering the cover building, it is important to appreciate that only two areas of the baths provide the focus of the visible remains; that is the swimming pool (*natatio*) and the cold bath suite (*frigidarium*). A glance at the accompanying plans, together with the illuminating site graphics, should enable the visitor to place these remains in context with no great difficulty.

Plan of Fortress Baths
showing area of cover-building

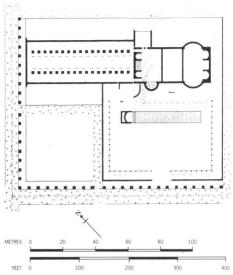

METRES 0 20 40 60 80 100

FEET 0 100 200 300 400

Roman Bathing — The Legionaries Relax

For the Romans, a bath building was not simply a public bath house. It combined the amenities of a modern leisure centre with something of the ambience of a gentleman's club. Here one could play ball games or gamble, meet one's friends, visit a masseur or a wine bar, buy a pasty, a mutton chop or a roast duck. At *Isca*, wine and beer were also probably served in the Fortress Baths. In Rome, the major bath buildings included art galleries, as well as Greek and Latin libraries, and could also cater for less elevated tastes. Women and small children also used the Caerleon baths, as is shown by the numerous hair pins and items of jewellery from the main drain of the Fortress Baths, along with a number of milk teeth. In some towns, local by-laws decreed that ladies should use the baths in the morning, men in the afternoon. Several emperors found it necessary to forbid mixed bathing, which suggests that it did sometimes take place, though perhaps not among respectable women.

A soldier of *Legio II Augusta* coming to the baths would strip, place his clothes in a locker under the care of one of the bath house slaves, and pass through into the *frigidarium* or cold bath suite. After a cold dip, he would anoint his body

with oils from a glass bath flask, a number of which have been found here during excavation. The legionary would then visit the warm and hot bath suites in turn. Heat from wood-burning furnaces, stoked by slaves, passed through hypocausts, where rows of brick piers supported a raised floor to give underfloor heating. Additional warmth was transmitted through pottery heating ducts in the walls. Lead boiler tanks over the furnaces provided hot water.

The oil and sweat would be scraped from the bather's body with a metal scraper or strigil. One visitor to the baths was unlucky enough to lose one of a pair of expensive strigils, richly inlaid with silver, gold and brass, and decorated with the twelve labours of Hercules, which eventually found its way into the bath house drain where it was recovered on excavation. Bathers often wore their rings and other jewellery in the baths

(pilfering from lockers was not unknown), and the wet heat sometimes loosened gemstones from rings, or even the ring itself from the bather's finger. Amongst a host of small objects swept into the bath house drain was a remarkable collection of 88 engraved gemstones of amethyst, cornelian, jasper and other stones (see Further Reading p. 47 for a separate booklet on these gemstones). Other small objects recovered from the drain help to fill out our picture of life in the baths: counters for

When excavated, the main drain of the Fortress Baths — large enough to walk upright in — contained a wealth of objects illustrating the daily life of the building and its users (By permission of the National Museum of Wales).

The collection of 88 engraved Roman gemstones from the drain of the Fortress Baths. They are now in the Legionary Museum (By permission of the National Museum of Wales).

gaming, bone hair pins, together with animal and bird bones and an olive stone from the snacks sold to bathers.

After his hot bath, the legionary would return through the warm and cold rooms, take a final cold dip, and perhaps visit the latrine. He would then dress and return to the baths *basilica* or to the courtyard to watch the ball players, or simply to talk with friends.

The Scale of the Bath Building

Inside the modern cover-building, the visitor will begin to appreciate the impressive scale of the baths structure. The site exhibition and illustrations, including reconstructions, spoken commentaries and computer graphics, have been prepared by the National Museum of Wales and may be consulted independently of this guidebook.

Plan of the Fortress Baths
showing principal features in the cover-building

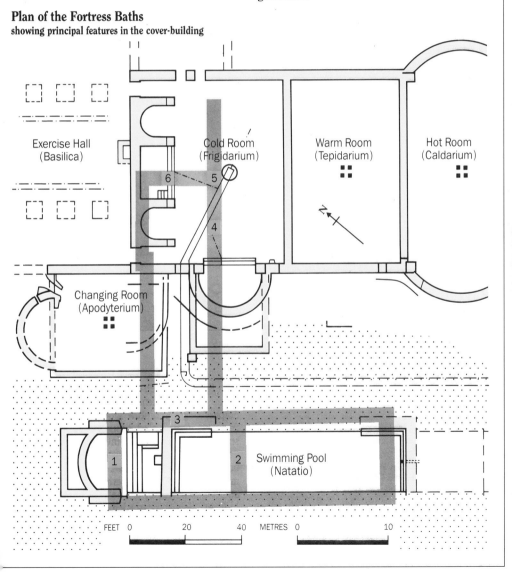

Exercise Hall (Basilica)

Cold Room (Frigidarium)

Warm Room (Tepidarium)

Hot Room (Caldarium)

Changing Room (Apodyterium)

Swimming Pool (Natatio)

FEET 0   20   40   METRES 0   10

The baths were built around A.D. 80, on a space reserved for them when the fortress was established a few years before. The massive construction of stone and concrete would have towered over the remainder of the fortress, which at this time was built almost entirely of timber. Concrete, and the wide vaulted spans it made possible, were still fairly novel at the time. There was room for architects and engineers to experiment, and the superstructure and vault of the Fortress Baths may have resembled the surviving *frigidarium* of the Cluny Baths in Paris.

The Cluny Baths, which survive as part of one of Paris's major museums, show how the Caerleon Fortress Baths may once have looked (By courtesy of Musée des Thermes et de l'Hôtel de Cluny, Paris).

The building may indeed have anticipated the design of the great Imperial Baths of Rome itself; notably in the symmetrical planning and vaulted domes.

In scale, and to some extent in plan, the Fortress Baths can be compared to a medieval cathedral, with its aisled *basilica* matching the nave, and the three halls of the bath suite the chancel. The overall length of some 360 feet (110m) equals that of Wells Cathedral and is only slightly less than, for example, Durham at 425 feet (130m). In turn, the vaulted domes of the bath suite would have been at roughly the height of the roof vault in a later cathedral.

The Natatio or Swimming Bath

The first structure the visitor now encounters within the cover-building would have been originally a swimming bath in the open air. It stood at the end of the courtyard between the baths and the main street, with the principal wall of the bath building proper rising behind it. Supplied with a continuous flow of water through lead pipes, it held some 80,250 gallons (365,000 lt) and was 135 feet (41m) long, with a larger surface area than the Great Bath at *Aquae Sulis*, Bath.

At one end (left as the visitor enters) ⬛ was a half round fountain house or *nymphaeum*, with the foundation of its apse still visible. Examples

The apse of the natatio (swimming bath) fountain house, demolished when the pool was shortened.

from Pompeii and elsewhere suggest that this would have been richly decorated. Part of a stone dolphin from a sculpture group survives, and fragments of wall plaster found during excavation show that the apse was painted with a colourful aquatic or garden scene. Water, from a tank behind the apse, would have gushed from the mouth of the dolphin — perhaps one of a pair — and possibly from an urn held by a central figure. In front, the water cascaded down a flight of steps clad in broad slabs of Purbeck marble, parts of which remain *in situ*. These steps did not give access to the pool and later, steps for bathers were provided at one side.

From the shallow end, some 4 feet (1.2m) deep, the water shelved to about 5½ feet (1.6m) at the deep end. The walls of the *natatio* were built of flanged roofing tiles set in mortar, with a waterproof cement rendering on the face. Originally, the floor was of concrete mixed with crushed brick (the present red gravel is modern).

Around A.D. 110, the baths were refurbished and the floor and sides of the pool were lined with flagstones, though in turn these were removed in a later phase; only traces of their impressions in the mortar bed remain. About forty years later, the pool was radically altered. The fountain house appears to have been prone to subsidence, and was now demolished, though the sculpture group was perhaps set up elsewhere. The pool itself was shortened by building two blocking walls across it and filling-in behind. The length of the *natatio* was thus reduced from 135 feet (41m) to just 84 feet (25.5m).

An artists impression of the shortened natatio, *with the marble clad steps and demolished apse behind (Illustration by John Banbury, after Zienkiewicz 1986).*

The blocking wall of the shortened natatio *from the rear.*

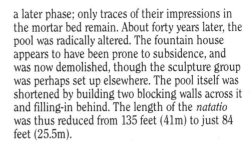

An artist's impression of the fountain house as it may have appeared when first built. Similar structures survive intact at Pompeii and elsewhere (Illustration by John Banbury, after Zienkiewicz 1986).

A stone dolphin head, probably part of a sculptural group from the fountain house apse.

A Bird's-Eye View of Caerleon from the North-West

showing the principal Roman remains in relation to the modern town

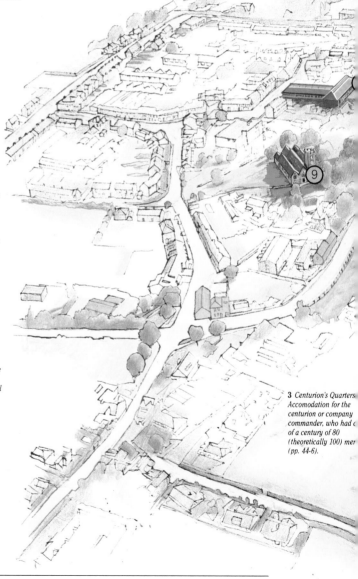

7 *Fortress Baths — Inside the modern-cover building are parts of a monumental bath complex on the scale of a medieval cathedral, built very soon after the Second Augustan Legion arrived at Caerleon about A.D. 75. An outdoor swimming pool, the cold bath suite and a heated changing room can be seen (pp. 18-23, 26-30).*

12 *Roman Legionary Museum — The museum houses important collections of artefacts excavated at many sites in and around the fortress, including the Fortress Baths, the Prysg Field barracks and the amphitheatre.*

9 *St Cadoc's Church — The church and churchyard overlie the legionary headquarters building, where the regimental standards were kept in their shrine (pp. 12, 15).*

3 *Centurion's Quarters Accomodation for the centurion or company commander, who had c of a century of 80 (theoretically 100) mer (pp. 44-6).*

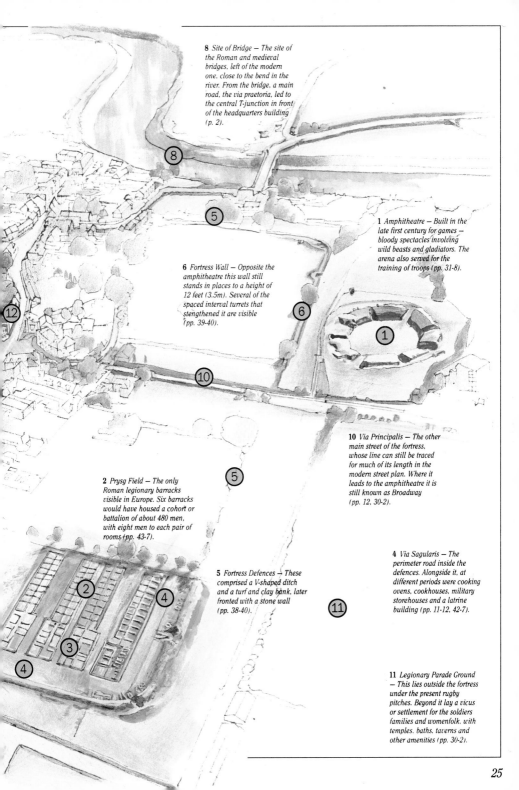

8 *Site of Bridge* — The site of the Roman and medieval bridges, left of the modern one, close to the bend in the river. From the bridge, a main road, the *via praetoria*, led to the central T-junction in front of the headquarters building (p. 2).

1 *Amphitheatre* — Built in the late first century for games — bloody spectacles involving wild beasts and gladiators. The arena also served for the training of troops (pp. 31-8).

6 *Fortress Wall* — Opposite the amphitheatre this wall still stands in places to a height of 12 feet (3.5m). Several of the spaced interval turrets that stengthened it are visible (pp. 39-40).

10 *Via Principalis* — The other main street of the fortress, whose line can still be traced for much of its length in the modern street plan. Where it leads to the amphitheatre it is still known as Broadway (pp. 12, 30-2).

2 *Prysg Field* — The only Roman legionary barracks visible in Europe. Six barracks would have housed a cohort or battalion of about 480 men, with eight men to each pair of rooms (pp. 43-7).

4 *Via Sagularis* — The perimeter road inside the defences. Alongside it, at different periods were cooking ovens, cookhouses, military storehouses and a latrine building (pp. 11-12, 42-7).

5 *Fortress Defences* — These comprised a V-shaped ditch and a turf and clay bank, later fronted with a stone wall (pp. 38-40).

11 *Legionary Parade Ground* — This lies outside the fortress under the present rugby pitches. Beyond it lay a *vicus* or settlement for the soldiers families and womenfolk, with temples, baths, taverns and other amenities (pp. 30-2).

This new short pool was lined with sandstone slabs, but these too were later removed. The north-west blocking wall, of stone and red tile, with a strengthening buttress behind it, can be seen (near entrance of cover-building), with steps for bathers in front of it. The fill behind has been removed, and this enables us to see the original length of the pool, along with the foundation of the fountain house apse.

From the viewing platform which crosses the width of the *natatio* **2**, the visitor will see at the opposite end the outer face of the other blocking wall. Again, there are steps in front, and it still has its lead outlet pipe.

The outlet pipe at the lower end of the shortened swimming bath.

It was perhaps at the time of the renovation of *Isca* (above, pp. 15-16) under Septimius Severus (A.D. 193-211) that the stone slabs lining the pool were removed. They were perhaps needed for more urgent repairs elsewhere in the fortress. Later, the pool was given a new cement lining, and although less grand it continued in use until about A.D. 240.

An artist's impression of soldiers removing the stone lining slabs of the swimming bath during the rebuilding of the fortress under Septimus Severus, about A.D. 200. The slabs were probably needed for reuse on another building (Illustration by John Banbury, after Zienkiewicz 1986).

The Bath Building – Heated Changing Room (Apodyterium)

The coarse gravel set around the swimming pool, though modern, shows the area of the open-air courtyard (*palaestra*) in which it stood. If the visitor now turns from the *natatio*, to consider the other long axis of the cover-building, beyond the coarse gravel we may next consider the concrete and stone remains of the bath building itself **3**.

The remains at this end (nearest the *natatio*) include a heated changing room (*apodyterium*)

The remains of the apodyterium or heated changing room, showing the pillars of the hypocaust or underfloor central heating.

and a cold plunge bath. The changing room can be seen at basement level to the left, and is distinguished by the rows of small, square brick pillars from a hypocaust or underfloor heating system. To the right, with its curved edge, is the paved floor of the plunge bath. Between these is the crown of the main bath house drain, which can be seen where it turns at the edge of the courtyard. Many of the brick pillars in the

The crown of the main bath house drain, seen turning at what was once the edge of a courtyard.

changing room have been robbed out in later centuries, leaving little more than their impressions in the concrete bed.

A heated room in which to undress would have been appreciated by a soldier of *Legio II Augusta*, facing the rigours of a Welsh winter. In its present form, the changing room was an addition to the bath halls, and was built around A.D. 150. Excavation outside the cover-building (to the left) has shown that it had a large apse in its end wall and replaced an earlier heated room on the same site. There would have been rows of wooden lockers for clothes around the walls. Bathers may have worn wooden sandals because of the heat from the floor, and after undressing they would have gone through into the *frigidarium* or cold bath suite.

There were almost certainly other changing rooms situated around the *frigidarium*, and the mosaic now on the end (far) wall of the cover-building, found within a few feet of its present position in 1877, probably came from one such chamber.

A painting of the mosaic fragment found in 1877 under Back Hall Street. It shows the tip of a ceremonial wand of the god Bacchus. The original is now on display at the Fortress Baths (By permission of the National Museum of Wales).

An artist's impression of the heated changing room as it might once have looked. The lockers and seats are based on surviving marble examples from Italy, but the statue and wall decoration are hypothetical (Illustration by John Banbury, after Zienkiewicz 1986)

The Bath Building – Cold Bath Hall (Frigidarium)

The thick wall beyond the heated changing room was initially the main external wall of the bath building, before the addition of the later changing room. At this end, the remains we see are those of part of the cold bath hall ▦ (*frigidarium*). However, only half of this can now be seen. It extends outside the cover-building, where, below the modern gardens and houses, the remains lead on to the warm and hot halls. The entire bath suite thus continued on to the right, and in fact was six times the length of the visible remains.

The end (left) wall of the cold hall was a massive block of solid masonry, taking some of the weight and thrust of the concrete vaults above. In

The apses at the end of the cold hall would originally have held a central cold bath and a pair of flanking basins for a cold splash bath, as in the illustration below.

An impression of the frigidarium or cold bath suite as it might once have been. It is interesting to compare this illustration with the surviving Cluny Baths, p. 22 (Illustration by John Banbury, after Zienkiewicz 1986).

this wall, at ground level, were triple recesses, comprising a central rectangular bath flanked by semi-circular recesses. There was a similar arrangement at the opposite end of the bath suite, forming the end wall of the hot bath hall (*caldarium*). When first built, the two apsidal alcoves housed a pair of circular basins on high pedestals, in which bathers could splash down. Part of a similar basin (*labrum*) in Purbeck marble, decorated with a gorgon's head, found at

Artist's impression of soldiers of the Second Legion enjoying a cold shower (Illustration by John Banbury).

This Purbeck marble basin was found in the nineteenth century at a bath house outside the fortress walls. Decorated with a Gorgon's head, it was used for cold splash baths (see reconstruction drawing opposite).

another Caerleon bath house, has been set up next to one of the alcoves to illustrate the size and shape of these basins. Later, the alcoves were turned into additional cold pools, the plaster linings and half-round angle mouldings of which survive remarkably intact. The rectangular basin between them still has part of its lining of sandstone slabs.

To the right of these recesses, the bath hall had a floor of large rectangular stone flags, parts of which remain. Here bathers would have stood after a visit to the *caldarium*, whilst attendants would have thrown buckets of water over them. Consequently, the floor was given a slight downwards slope towards its centre, where there was a circular perforated cover over a drain which carried off the splashed water. Any overflow from the baths would also be carried into an underlying drain. The position of this drain cover may be seen in a recess (on the opposite side of

the walkway) in the right-hand wall of the cover building **5**. The circular cover is gone, but one stone of its surround, cut to a curve, remains. A similar drain cover, found at one of the other

Drain cover from the 'Castle Baths', outside the fortress walls at Caerleon, excavated in the nineteenth century and now exhibited in the Fortress Baths.

Caerleon bath houses in the nineteenth century, is exhibited nearby. Below the drain hole itself, a light shows the underlying brick-built *frigidarium* drain.

At the end of the *frigidarium*, a double doorway led through to a second heated chamber **6**. This now lies under Backhall Street to the rear of the cover-building. Part of the first-century mosaic pavement from this, found under the street in 1877, has been placed on the end wall. The surviving part shows the end of a Bacchic wand or *thyrsus*, originally borne by devotees of the god Bacchus or Dionysus (see illustration on p. 27). In the complete pavement it seems likely that two such wands were crossed over a large circular device, possibly a shield.

The End of the Bath Building

As we have seen the Fortress Baths appear to have been maintained for use by the legion until *c.* A.D. 230-40. The surfaces within the building seem generally to have been kept free of rubbish until about A.D. 270, but after that time all hope of reopening the baths was apparently given up. This enormous building did, however, survive as a shell until the twelfth or thirteenth century.

In front of the triple recesses at the end of the cold hall (*frigidarium*), the visitor will notice a row of regularly-spaced ragged pits. These show where piers built of large blocks of dressed masonry, like those surviving in the main entrance of the amphitheatre (pp. 34-5), were robbed out in medieval times. In the intervening centuries, with the roof and vaults intact, the bath building had become the haunt of barn owls (as an examination of rodent remains from the excavations has shown), who often roost in derelict roofed structures.

We should not be surprised that such a formidable construction could survive for so long. Indeed, the Cluny Baths in Paris still stand with the *frigidarium* vault intact as part of one of the major museums of the city. Perhaps all that prevented the Fortress Baths from surviving to our own day in a similar condition was a shortage of building stone, which led the builders of Caerleon Castle or one of the medieval monastic houses of the area to pillage the Baths to meet their needs.

The Amphitheatre

The road from the Legionary Museum and church down to the amphitheatre, known as Broadway, follows one of the main streets of the Roman fortress, the *via principalis*. Where the modern road opens out as it approaches the amphitheatre, the *via principalis* passed through

An aerial view of the amphitheatre from the south.

one of the fortress gates, before continuing down through the civilian settlement outside the walls to quays and wharfs on the River Usk. The gateway stood mid way along one of the four sides of the fortress defences. Looking back along Broadway towards the museum, the visitor will gain some impression of the size of the legionary fortress as a whole.

The amphitheatre during the very early stages of excavation — 'King Arthur's Round Table'.

To the right, behind the amphitheatre, the fortress wall continues down to the southern angle of the defences. To the left, a grassy scarp on a hedgeline marks the line of the now vanished wall as it ran towards the Prysg Field barracks at the west angle. The church tower, among the trees, stands at the centre of the fortress, over the *principia* or headquarters building. To the immediate right is the amphitheatre itself, whilst to the left, the Caerleon Rugby Club pitch is on the site of the parade ground of the Second Augustan Legion.

The Building and Appearance of the Amphitheatre

The soldiers of the legion, originally recruited from Italy, Provence and southern Spain, would expect, even in this relatively bleak frontier base, to be provided with some of the amenities of home. The Fortress Baths were, as we have seen, planned on a generous scale from the outset. Moreover, within the first generation of the fortress another bath building was constructed outside the defences, perhaps for the inhabitants of the settlement catering for the needs of the soldiers which sprang up below the walls. Around A.D. 90, however, it was decided to provide the legion with an amphitheatre. Space was limited, much of it already taken up by the civilian

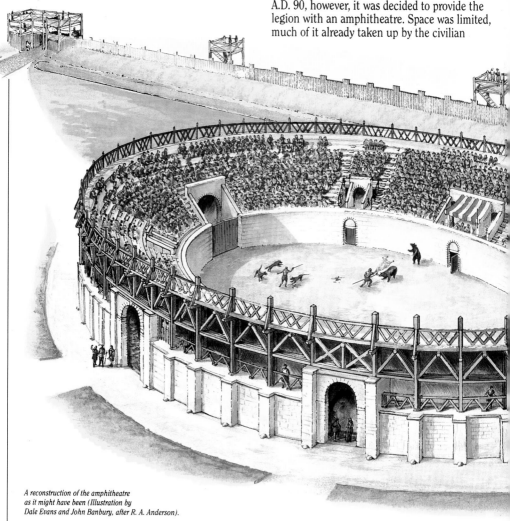

A reconstruction of the amphitheatre as it might have been (Illustration by Dale Evans and John Banbury, after R. A. Anderson).

'Third cohort, century of Rufinus Primus' — one of the inscriptions from the amphitheatre, recording the units of the legion which took part in its building (By permission of the National Museum of Wales).

settlement, by storage sheds and an extra-mural bath building. Eventually room was found between the fortress defences and the extra-mural

bath building, but even so it was necessary to rebuild one corner of the baths to avoid blocking one of the amphitheatre entrances. The siting of the amphitheatre in this position shows that no real trouble was now expected from the Silures. It obstructs the field of fire from the fortress walls, and in turn would have given cover to attackers.

Inside and out, the amphitheatre would have looked very like a modern provincial Spanish bullring. The lower part was of stone, well buttressed to resist the earth banking, which was never higher than we see today. The upper part was a timber openwork grandstand, perhaps intended as a temporary measure, though never replaced in stone. Inside was an oval arena (the word means 'sand' in both Latin and Spanish), surrounded with the banks of wooden seating. There were two major entrances or *portae pompae*, through which the procession of fighters would enter the arena at the beginning of the games, saluting the president — the legionary legate or distinguished visitor — seated in a box above one of the side entrances. Six lesser entrances were spaced around the arena and these allowed spectators to gain access to their seats, and performers (animal or human) access to the central arena. The timber grandstand housed around 6,000 seats, slightly more than the full complement of the legion.

The legionary stonemasons who, with its carpenters, built the amphitheatre, recorded their work on inscribed stones naming the century responsible for a particular wall. This would also serve as a form of quality control. Several of these were found during the excavations directed by Mortimer Wheeler in 1926-27, and copies can be seen in the display by the sales office. They begin *7*(century of) followed by the name of the centurion and sometimes the number of his cohort. Also displayed at the sales office are tiles with the legionary title LEG II AUG, and some with footprints of men and animals who trod on the bricks as they lay out to dry in the brickyard.

A Tour of the Amphitheatre

From the sales office, the visitor can walk down into the arena through the north entrance (**F** on plan), one of a pair of processional entries (*portae pompae*) planned parallel with the long axis. The outer part of this entry was barrel-vaulted in stone, but the inner half was unroofed and open to the sky. The jambs of dressed freestone, which supported the vault, survive to their full height.

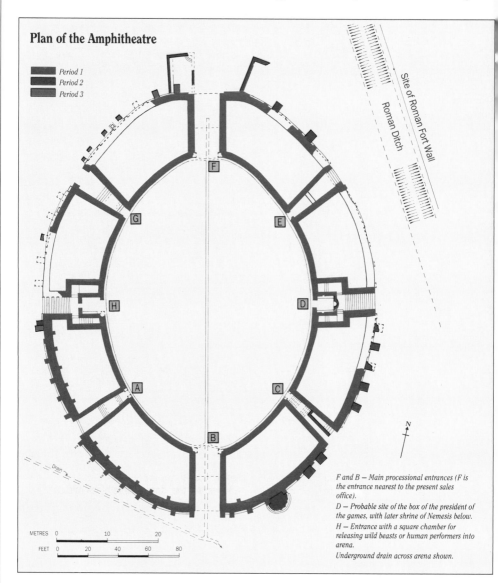

Plan of the Amphitheatre

Period 1
Period 2
Period 3

Site of Roman Fort Wall

Roman Ditch

F
G
E
H
D
A
C
B

N

F and B — Main processional entrances (F is the entrance nearest to the present sales office).

D — Probable site of the box of the president of the games, with later shrine of Nemesis below.

H — Entrance with a square chamber for releasing wild beasts or human performers into arena.

Underground drain across arena shown.

METRES 0   10   20

FEET 0   20   40   60   80

Drain

One of the main entrances – (portae pompae) to the arena (F). Through these, a procession of performers would enter at the beginning of the games and salute the president of the games in his box.

to the arena. Here, gladiators or prisoners would await their turn, and wild beasts would be penned before being released into the roar of the arena. One of the staircases in entrance **D** (that on the left with the brick apse) is wider and probably led up to the box of the president of the games situated above the entrance itself.

During the history of the fortress, the amphitheatre was repaired from time to time. The external buttresses were rebuilt or renewed and the spaces at the bottom of all the entrances except the *portae pompae* were filled in, thereby burying the lower parts of the steps (this filling has now been removed). Entrances **D** and **H** on the short axis were more radically altered.

Entrance **H** (on the right) is very well preserved. At the bottom of the entrance steps, the brick arch under which spectators turned

In the opposite (southern, **B**) entrance, collapsed arch stones of the vault were found lying where they had fallen. Some of the Roman paving of the northern entrance survives, now protected by a rail. A large drain runs under the entrance, across the arena, and out through the southern *portae pompae*. It still drains the arena very effectively in wet weather.

In Roman times, the present grass surface would have been sand or fine gravel, giving a secure foothold to the gladiators and beast hunters, to whom a slipped foot would often have been fatal. Around the arena, a shallow drain carries off the surface water and behind this are the remains of the arena wall. This was once finished with a surface of smooth white plaster, and was crowned with a heavy stone coping carrying a rail. Above this on the banking, which was never any higher than it is today, were the tiers of wooden seats; traces of these uprights have been found in excavation.

The spectator, with a 'ticket' (in the form of a lead token), would approach via one of the six lesser entrances, passing down a flight of stairs and up another at the side, out on to the banking where the seats were probably numbered. The two side entrances (**D** and **H** on plan) parallel with the short axis of the arena were larger. Each had a pair of flanking staircases up to the terrace, on either side of a small, square central room which had access both from the outside staircase and on

Entrance H, which includes a chamber or pen from which performers would be released into the arena.

right to reach the steps up to the banking still survives; so, too, does a large block of stone, originally from the barrel vault of the entrance, which was carefully set into the angle of the passage during later alterations, perhaps for a steward or ticket collector. The left-hand stair (looking into the amphitheatre) was blocked and filled in at the same time. The brick rear wall of the beast pen opening on to the arena also survives. The line of its original barrel vault and door can be seen marked on the brickwork, together with the line of a later altered doorway. During the renovations in the early third century, under Severus or Caracalla (pp. 15-16), the entrance was filled in level with the ground outside, burying and so preserving the earlier features we can see today.

Directly opposite, entrance **D** also shows alterations. Here, the broad stair, which probably

Entrance D, with the brick apse of the shrine of Nemesis. The box of the president of the games would be above this.

led to the president's box, was blocked and filled in. The entry from the staircase to the animal pen or waiting room for gladiators was also blocked, so that this could now only be reached from the arena; a cupboard-like feature was inserted in its rear wall. Later, as with entrance **H** , this entry was filled in level with the surrounding ground and the brick niche was inserted in the rear wall of the chamber. On excavation, many of its bricks were found to be stamped LEG II AUG ANTO, using the title 'Antoninus' (Caracalla's) Own', held by the legion from A.D. 211-17. In these later phases, this chamber may have been used as a shrine of Nemesis, the goddess of fate and divine vengeance, who punished crime.

Shrines to Nemesis are known at other amphitheatres, including Chester, and here at

Caerleon a lead plaque found in the arena carries a scratched dedication to the goddess, asking for a

'To the Goddess Nemesis, I give you this cloak and these boots . . .' A lead curse tablet found near entrance D (By permission of the National Museum of Wales).

curse on an un-named person. The story behind this is not wholly clear, but it was common for the victim of a theft to dedicate either the stolen object, or the thief, to a god or goddess, in return for vengeance. In this case, a cloak and a pair of

In addition to the games held as part of important festivals, the amphitheatre would also have been used for regular military training or weapon demonstrations (Illustration by Peter Connolly).

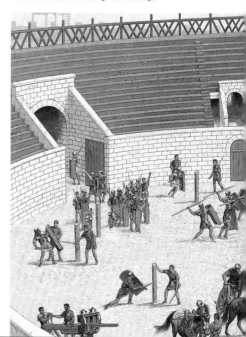

boots were involved and the writer of the curse, who may have been a gladiator, seems to be wishing ill upon the (? unknown) thief, whom he perhaps suspected was another gladiator — 'May he not redeem them, save with his life blood'.

Games would usually be part of a religious or military festival, much as a saint's day may be celebrated today with bulls in some countries. After the hard work of a ceremonial parade to celebrate the legion's birthday (23 September), that of the emperor or those of past emperors of good repute (who were regarded as gods), the soldiers could look forward to the entertainment offered by the amphitheatre. Top gladiators were expensive, just as their present day musical or sporting counterparts are, but a 'star' name might be hired for a special occasion; there was perhaps no shortage of lesser performers or even amateurs from within the legion. Cheaper still were condemned criminals, sentenced to the beasts, or to fight with the gladiators. Lions or leopards would rarely be seen at Caerleon, if at all, but the local forests could provide bears, wild boars or wolves, and bulls and even cows were often used in the arena. Other animals, such as deer, might be hunted on horseback in *venationes* or mounted hunts.

This early fifth-century ivory from Rome is the left leaf of a diptych. It shows a president and two others presiding over an elk fight in an amphitheatre (By courtesy of Merseyside County Museums, Liverpool).

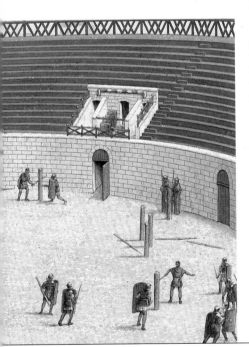

Of the human victims, the fullest accounts are of condemned Christians, for the endurances of these 'athletes of Christ' were recorded by their fellow believers. We have, for example, the prison diary of Vibia Perpetua, a young married woman from Carthage (in modern Tunisia), who was killed in the arena there, with a group of her fellow Christians, to celebrate the birthday of the emperor Geta in A.D. 203. There is no evidence, however, that any Christian martyrs suffered in the Caerleon amphitheatre. The two Caerleon martyrs, Julius and Aaron, if legionaries (and therefore Roman citizens), would have been beheaded rather than subjected to the sadistic indignities of the arena.

The amphitheatre could also be used for military training or weapon demonstrations, and as a place where the legion could be assembled for a speech from its commander or a visiting dignitary. It is no coincidence that it stood next to the parade ground, which would have had a saluting base for similar, but more formal occasions.

Leaving the amphitheatre by the main south entrance (B on plan), the visitor will notice the massive freestone piers supporting the vault over its outer half, still standing to their full height.

The outside wall of the amphitheatre was solidly butressed to resist the thrust of the earth fill.

Turning right and returning towards the ticket office, we may observe the well-preserved buttressed exterior. Stone slabs, set like bollards, can be seen near some of the buttresses, and these were to prevent damage by vehicles using the perimeter road. On the left, near entrance H, the furnace and a corner of the large first-century bath building can be seen. It pre-dated the

This corner of a large first-century bath building — earlier than the amphitheatre — was altered when the latter was built, since it obstructed one of the entrances.

amphitheatre but was remodelled when the latter was built, so that it did not block the adjacent entrance or the perimeter road. It is now shown in its altered state.

Visitors should now leave the site and return to Broadway, to the point where the modern road broadens out as it approaches the amphitheatre car-park.

The South-West Fortress Defences

The modern road outside the amphitheatre site is on the line of the Roman road from the south-west gate of the fortress to the river. On the right, behind the amphitheatre, the line of the Roman defences can be seen as a low stone wall, with higher ground to its rear. The wall runs down from near the road to the southern angle of the fortress. It has been much robbed for building stone in past centuries. The squared blocks of sandstone with which it was once faced are now mostly gone, leaving the rubble core exposed.

Originally the defences comprised a turf and clay bank with a front revetment of wooden posts,

An aerial view of the early-second century fortress wall near the amphitheatre. Its present state is due to stone robbing rather than age.

a timber gate with twin towers flanking a central entrance, and a series of timber towers at spaced intervals (see illustrations, pp. 10-11, 40-1). About A.D. 100-10, these timber defences were replaced by a stone wall 5 feet (1.5m) thick, fronting the original bank (now represented by the higher ground inside the wall), a twin-towered stone gate and a series of stone turrets at intervals of about 46 yards (43m).

Where the modern road broadens out as it approaches the amphitheatre, the south-west gate spanned the Roman road (as it does the modern) out of the fortress. Of its two flanking towers, that on the left has been excavated (though nothing is visible today). It projected from the line of the wall, in a way characteristic of later Roman gateways, and may have rebuilt in the early third century, for an inscription of Caracalla (A.D. 212-17) was found nearby in 1603. The right-hand tower lies under the small walled yard by the roadside, and awaits excavation.

A Tour of the Defences

An often muddy public footpath, reached over a stile, follows the line of the ditch in front of the fortress wall down to its southern angle. A gravelled walk can be followed along the top of the wall. Until a few years ago, the Roman wall was partly hidden by a Victorian facing. This has now been removed and the Roman stonework conserved. Of the three internal turrets along this stretch of wall, two are unexcavated. Their positions are known, but the evidence they contain has been left intact for the future. The wall in front of the third turret has been entirely robbed out, exposing the interior.

The basement of one of the series of turrets that guarded the fortress wall. The front wall of the turret has been removed by stone robbers.

The towers were of two storeys, the lower being a virtual basement, built into the bank and serving only to support the first floor and battlemented roof above it. The ground floor was reached through a door in its rear wall and was used, perhaps illicitly, for dumping ashes and rubbish from the cooking ovens to the rear. When found, it was filled with 5 feet (1.5m) of ashes and clay, rich in occupation debris. In the mid second century, a cookhouse, like those to be seen in the Prysg Field (p. 42), was added behind. This has not, however, been excavated and the doorway to the rear of the turret has been blocked off, with a datestone to show that this is modern masonry.

Inside the southern angle, the corner turret, originally excavated in 1909, has been exposed and conserved. The legion's masons had trouble with the wall here due to subsidence. Several settlement cracks can be seen on the outside of the wall, which shows substantial signs of rebuilding. Inside the angle was a latrine, like that

in the Prysg Field, but this is not now visible. This corner of the fortress was used in World War II for a brick rifle position, covering the bridge, but regrettably it has been necessary to remove this relic of more recent history in order to conserve the Roman wall.

The wall itself still stands to a height of around 12 feet (3.5m) at the rounded southern angle, though it is necessary to retrace one's steps to see this impressive work from outside. As elsewhere, the facework has been robbed out, but the brick fragments and the crushed brick in the mortar show where it has been rebuilt in Roman times. A number of 'putlog' holes for the wooden scaffolding used to build the wall can be seen, and just past the angle is a brick-arched drain, from the inside of the fortress, which originally discharged into the ditch.

Leaving the defences in this southern corner of the fortress, following the footpath acrosss the field, the visitor may walk up the main street back to the Fortress Baths. Otherwise, one can reach the Prysg Field barracks by returning to the road

The clay and turf fortress rampart, seen in section during excavation (By courtesy of Howard Mason).

At its southern angle, the fortress wall stands to a height of some twelve feet (3.5m). The holes for the scaffolding used to build it can still be seen.

near the amphitheatre and following the footpath on the opposite side, where the grassy scarp on the hedgeline to the right marks the vanished defences. The broad hollow in front of this is on the line of the ditch, but its profile is due to the footpath and bears no relationship to the actual Roman ditch. A gravel path over this hollow leads, through a gate, to the Prysg Field Barracks.

The Prysg Field Barracks

Dr V.E. Nash-Williams's excavations here, in 1927-29, uncovered a row of barrack buildings, each of which had housed a legionary century, with its centurion. Similar barracks have been excavated in various parts of the Roman Empire, but these are the only legionary barrack blocks now visible in Europe. As its name implies, each century at one time comprised 100 men, but by the time *Isca* was established the complement had become 80. A century was divided into ten groups of eight men, each group sharing a pair of rooms in the barrack block. This arrangement was derived from conditions on campaign, when eight men would share a rectangular tent, the tents of each century being pitched in a line, with the larger tent of the centurion and his staff at the end.

The centuries, or infantry companies, were grouped into cohorts, or battalions, each of about 500 men — six centuries of 80 men apiece, making a total of 480. There were ten cohorts in the legion, so that 60 barrack blocks of the type seen in the Prysg Field would be needed for the entire legion (bearing in mind the complications

The arrangement of permanent barrack blocks was derived from campaign conditions, when eight soldiers shared a rectangular tent (Illustration by Peter Connolly).

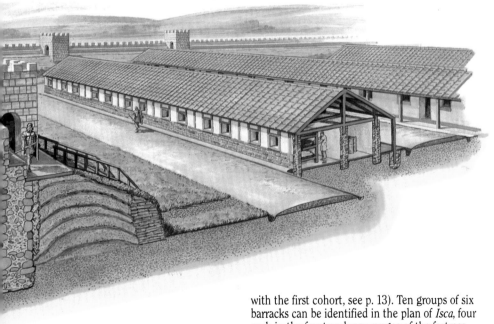

An artist's impression of the Prysg Field barracks as they may have appeared in the early second century (compare with illustration on pp. 10-11). The defences are now of stone, and the barracks half-timbered on stone sleeper walls (Illustration by John Banbury, after Howard Mason).

with the first cohort, see p. 13). Ten groups of six barracks can be identified in the plan of *Isca*, four each in the front and rear ranges of the fortress, and the two remaining cohorts, including the first, flanking each side of the headquarters building in the central zone.

The Defences, Ovens and Cookhouses

Immediately inside the entrance gate, the visitor will see that the Prysg Field barracks are situated within the western angle of the fortress. Before turning to consider the details, there are several features along the line of the defences which repay examination.

From the gate, the earth rampart of the defences runs down towards the angle. The wall in front of it has been entirely robbed out. The space between the rampart and the perimeter road (the *via sagularis*) was used for cooking, and a number of circular oven bases can be seen. There is a stone tower, like that behind the amphitheatre, mid way between the gate and the angle, with another in the far corner. Both of these towers had cookhouses added behind them in the mid second century. These have raised platforms inside, probably the bases for ovens and cooking hearths. To their rear, the broad *via*

The bases of circular ovens, used for cooking food, in the Prysg Field.

sagularis or perimeter road was designed to give rapid access to the ramparts, should the need arise, as well as facilitating the movements of bodies of troops. A drain separates this road from the first of the barrack blocks.

A coin of Severus Alexander (A.D. 222-35), found in excavations at the Prysg Field (By permission of the National Museum of Wales).

The four Prysg Field barracks from the air — the only Roman legionary barracks on display in Europe.

Plan of the Prysg Field Barracks

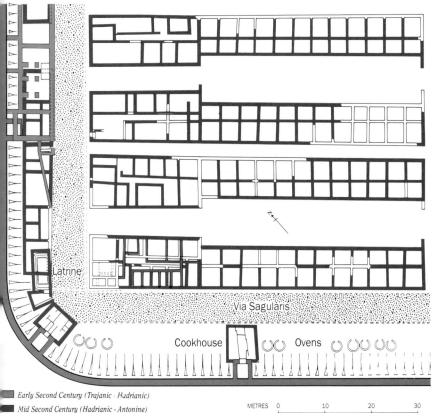

Latrine

Via Sagularis

Cookhouse 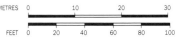 Ovens

Early Second Century (Trajanic - Hadrianic)
Mid Second Century (Hadrianic - Antonine)
Mid Second Century (Antonine)
Early Third Century (Severan)

METRES 0   10   20   30

FEET 0   20   40   60   80   100

'Single Men in Barracks' – The Legionary Barrack Blocks

Only the first barrack block is of original Roman masonry. The others, at a higher level, are in effect 'plans in stone' — replicas of the originals and built above them. The method of excavation used in 1927-29 merely trenched the buildings, leaving much of the Roman deposit inside them intact. It was impossible to clear these for conservation without destroying the deposits which may hold important clues for our future understanding of Caerleon. When first built, the barracks were of timber, but wood rots rapidly in this damp soil. They were rebuilt at first on cobble footings and later, in the early second century, in stone.

The six barrack blocks of each cohort faced inwards in pairs, corresponding to the maniples or double centuries into which the cohort was divided for some purposes. The blocks are long narrow buildings with twelve pairs of rooms, each pair housing eight men, with a covered veranda running down the inner side of each block. At the end is the larger block of rooms housing the centurion. In theory, only ten rooms should be needed for the 80 men, but there are usually more. The extra rooms may have been needed for recruits or replacements on temporary secondment, or for *immunes* (clerks or craftsmen exempt from routine military chores because of their job) attached to the century for ration purposes. There may well have been various reasons why the actual strength of the century sometimes varied from its establishment strength of 80.

Of the pairs of rooms, the outer (smaller) one would be used for storing kit, and the inner, slightly larger, for sleeping. They would have been less crammed than it might appear, for army documents surviving from elsewhere in the empire show that some men would be on detached duty — pursuing thieves, for example, or escorting tax collectors. Those in barracks would be allocated daily jobs, such as guard duty, cookhouse fatigues, cutting stone or timber, amid a variety of other jobs. It was not unknown for centurions to take bribes from soldiers who wished to avoid the dirty or unpleasant jobs, and in March A.D. 107, Julius Apollinaris, a legionary serving in the east, wrote home to his mother — 'thanks be to Serapis that while the others are working hard all day cutting stones, I am now a company clerk and stand around all day doing nothing'.

'The Backbone of the Army' — The Centurion and his Quarters

The ten to a dozen rooms of the centurion's suite contrast with the meagre pair in which eight of his men had to live. However, it also served as a company office and may have housed the junior NCOs of the century. Tombstones of centurions show them in full regimentals, with their medals (or the Roman equivalents) up and carrying the vine stick which was their badge of office. 'Among the Romans', wrote a Greek historian, 'the vine branch is a mark of honour. And those who obtain it . . . become centurions'. It was, though, more than a simple badge of office, and was used freely on the backs of lazy or unfortunate soldiers.

An artist's impression of a section through a legionary barrack block. The inner room slept eight, with arms and equipment stored in the outer room (Illustration by John Banbury, after Howard Mason).

The centurion's block in one of the Prysg Field barracks.

to serve in *III Augusta* based in Algeria. In 46 years service he served in a total of thirteen legions.

The centurion's block may have looked not unlike a small modern office suite, with a central corridor and with rooms leading off, and a latrine at the end. In the first barrack, at the lower level, the block was rebuilt later in its history and several periods of work are now visible. The overall plan can be better appreciated, without

Centurions might expect to be posted anywhere in the empire. Petronius Fortunatus, for example, was posted to *II Augusta* from *X Gemina*, then stationed at Vienna, and left Isca

The centurion Marcus Favonius Facilis of the Twentieth Legion, on his tombstone from Colchester. He is seen in full dress uniform, with a vine stick in his hand — both a badge of office and an instrument of punishment (By courtesy of Colchester and Essex Museum).

this complication, by examining the higher level barracks. The occupants were no strangers to paperwork — daily rosters, ration receipts, pay records and the like all had to be dealt with. For this, they employed carefully prepared shavings of wood not unlike file cards in general format, on which they wrote in ink. Waxed tablets were also used for other purposes. A surviving record from Caerleon lists men cutting timber for building work. From elsewhere, both in Britain and the east, virtual archives survive, recording in detail many aspects of the daily life of the men of the Roman army.

The Latrine

In the western angle of the fortress, next to the corner turret, is a latrine. This was built about A.D. 150, an earlier rampart building being demolished to make way for it. The remains are those of a single rectangular room (the foundation across the middle belongs to the earlier building), with a drain around three sides of the interior. Over the drain there would have been a series of wooden seats, but we should not imagine any partitions or separate cubicles. In front of the drain is a gutter and this would have held vinegar. Here, the legionaries would have washed the sponges which served them for lavatory paper, and which would have been kept i

A reconstruction of the Prysg Field latrine. The form of the wooden seats is known from surviving marble examples at Mediteranean sites (Illustration by John Banbury, after Howard Mason).

tub of vinegar on the floor. The small room to ne side probably housed a water tank and the ushing arrangements.

he Prysg Field latrine today.

The North-West Rampart Buildings

On the far side of the Prysg Field, behind the enturions' quarters in the four barrack blocks, a urther series of buildings is known from excavation, though nothing is now visible. In the early second century there were originally six blocks (with two pairs built end to end) — one per double century, with what was probably a storeroom for one of the pairs of centuries at each end, small offices for the two quartermasters, and a central lobby. In the third century, these blocks were replaced by a continuous range of magazines or stores, some with what were probably the bases for raised tanks to collect rainwater from the roofs.

When excavated, the buildings contained quantities of weapons and military equipment, including chain mail, lance heads and spear heads, many arrowheads and pilum heads from long-stemmed javelins which were a characteristic weapon of the legionary soldier. There were iron caltrops — vicious spiked objects which could be strewn on the ground to lame both men and horses — sword fittings of bone and of bronze, and in one room someone had been making and repairing the composite bows with which archers in some army units were equipped under the late empire.

Further Reading

The standard work on the Roman fortress at Caerleon is G.C. Boon's *Isca: The Roman Legionary Fortress at Caerleon, Mon.*, 3rd ed (Cardiff 1972). This is now updated by the same author's *The Legionary Fortress of Caerleon-Isca: A Brief Account* (Caerleon 1987).

For individual sites, see:
Excavation reports on the Prysg Field by V.E. Nash-Williams, in *Archaeologia Cambrensis*, 86 (1931), 99-157; 87 (1932), 48-104 (the finds), 265-349 (the pottery).
R.E.M. Wheeler and T.V. Wheeler, 'The Roman Amphitheatre at Caerleon, Monmouthshire', *Archaeologia*, 78 (1928), 111-218.
J. David Zienkiewicz, *The Legionary Fortress Baths at Caerleon*, 2 vols. (Cardiff 1986).

Further useful background may be consulted in:
R.J. Brewer, *Caerleon-Isca: The Roman Legionary Museum* (Caerleon 1987).

R.G. Collingwood and R.P. Wright, *The Roman Inscriptions of Britain*, vol. i (Oxford 1965), where the inscriptions from Caerleon are collected.
M.G. Jarrett, 'Legio II Augusta in Britain', *Archaeologia Cambrensis*, 113 (1964), 47-63.
L. Keppie, *The Making of the Roman Army* (London 1984).
V.E. Nash-Williams, *The Roman Frontier in Wales*, 2nd ed, revised by M.G. Jarrett (Cardiff 1969).
G. Webster, *The Roman Imperial Army*, 3rd ed (London 1985).
I.A. Richmond, 'Trajans Army on Trajan's Column', *Papers of the British School at Rome*, 13 (1935), 1-40.
J. David Zienkiewicz, *Roman Gems from Caerleon* (Caerleon 1987).

Caer Rufeinig Caerllion – Crynodeb

Hanes

Saif tref Caerllion heddiw ar safle'r *Isca Rufeinig*, caer Ail Leng Augustus *(Legio II Augusta)*, a enwyd ar ôl Afon Wysg. Mae ei hadfeilion wedi denu ymwelwyr ers y ddeuddegfed ganrif ac yn ystod y trigain mlynedd diwethaf daethpwyd o hyd i gynllun y rhan fwyaf o'r gaer wrth gloddio. Gall y cyhoedd weld yr amffitheatr, barics Cae Prysg, Baddonau'r Gaer a rhan o'r amddiffynfeydd.

Yr oedd tua deg ar hugain o lengoedd yn y fyddin Rufeinig, a phob un yn cynnwys tua 5,500 o filwyr traed arfog gyda'r holl wasanaethau cynnal angenrheidiol. Enwyd *Legio II Augusta* ar ôl yr Ymerawdwr Augustus, y gŵr a'i ffurfiodd. Fe'i rheolwyd gan legad llengol, Rhufeiniwr bonheddig o deulu seneddol, gyda chymorth chwe swyddog o dras gymdeithasol is. Ond asgwrn cefn y lleng oedd y trigain canwriad, pob un yn rheoli cannwr o bedwar ugain gŵr.

Cymerodd *Legio II Augusta* ran yng ngoresgyniad Prydain o dan yr Ymerawdwr Claudius ac ymsefydlodd yng Nghaer Wysg (Exeter) am rai blynyddoedd. Fe'i symudwyd i Gaerllion gan Vespasian, y rhoddwyd i'w gadfridog, Sextus Julius Frontinus, y dasg o goncro llwyth rhyfelgar y Silwriaid 'gelyn ffyrnig ac ystyfnig, ar dir sydd bron yn gwbl amhosibl'. Llwyddasai'r Silwriaid i wrthsefyll y Rhufeiniaid am bron deg mlynedd ar hugain gan guro'r llengoedd sawl tro. Yr oedd yr ymgyrch newydd yn rhan o bolisi Vespasian, gŵr a enillasai enw iddo'i hun - cyn iddo ddod yn ymerawdwr - wrth ymladd yn erbyn y Brythoniaid a'r Iddewon ar ffiniau'r ymerodraeth.

Codwyd *Isca*, y gaer newydd, ar aber afon Wysg, sef man y gallai llongau ei gyrraedd â chyflenwadau milwrol. Fe'i codwyd o bren yn gyntaf ond yn raddol rhoddwyd cerrig mwy parhaol yn lle'r pren yn yr adeiladau a'r amddiffynfeydd. Ond ar ôl tawelu Silwria nid oedd angen presenoldeb milwrol mawr yma ac yn raddol fe anfonwyd unedau'r lleng i ogledd Prydain (lle bu iddynt helpu i godi Mur Hadrian) neu i ardaloedd eraill. O hynny ymlaen gorsaf gatrodol, yn hytrach na garsiwn milwrol llawn, fu *Isca* gan mwyaf, a byddai'r rhan fwyaf o'r lleng mewn mannau eraill.

Disgrifiad

Mae'r holl safleoedd Rhufeinig o fewn cyrraedd hwylus i'w gilydd. Maent oll, heblaw'r amffitheatr, y tu mewn i'r gaer bedronglog hanner can erw (20.2ha), ac fe safai'r amffitheatr yn union y tu allan i un o'r pyrth.

Safai Baddonau'r Gaer, a ddiogelir bellach o dan adeilad goruchuddio modern, yn ymyl canol y gaer. Yn wahanol i'r mwyafrif o'r adeiladau yn *Isca*, fe'i codwyd o gerrig o'r cychwyn cyntaf - fframwaith enfawr o gerrig a choncrid ar raddfa eglwys gadeiriol ganoloesol. Y darnau a arddangosir yw'r *natatio* neu'r baddon nofio a hanner *frigidarium* neu ystafelloedd y baddonau oer. Yr oedd y prif adeilad yn cynnwys neuadd ymarfer fawr a chyfres o dair neuadd a gynhwysai baddonau oer, cynnes a phoeth; fe âi'r ymdrochwyr o un i'r llall. Yr oedd y *natatio* y tu allan i'r adeilad, mewn cwrt sydd o dan y maes parcio presennol. Yr oedd llawer swyddogaeth i'r baddonau - yr un fath â chanolfan hamdden fodern. Nid mannau i ymdrochi'n unig oeddent.

Daliai'r amffitheatr 6,000 o bobl, ychydig yn fwy na'r lleng gyfan. Gwaith maen sylweddol a chadarn oedd y rhannau isaf, ac yr oedd ei ran uchaf, sydd bellach wedi diflannu, yn eisteddfa o seddau pren mewn cylch. Yn yr ymrysonfa byddai gladiatoriaid yn ymladd anifeiliaid gwyllt, gladiatoriaid eraill a throseddwyr a ddedfrydwyd i farwolaeth. Gellid defnyddio'r amffitheatr hefyd ar gyfer hyfforddiant ymladd ag arfau, neu fel man lle gellid casglu'r lleng ynghyd ar gyfer areithiau. Mae'n debyg yr edrychai fel cylch ymladd teirw modern yn Sbaen y tu mewn a'r tu allan.

Daliai barics Cae Prysg gannwr o bedwar ugain gŵr yr un, wyth gŵr i bob pâr o ystafelloedd, gyda grŵp mwy o ystafelloedd yn y pen ar gyfer y canwriad a swyddfa'r fintai. Dyma'r unig wersyll llengol sydd i'w weld yn Ewrop heddiw. Yma, a hefyd gyferbyn â'r amffitheatr, gellir gweld rhannau o fur a thyrrau amddiffynfeydd y gaer. Yng nghornel Cae Prysg ceir tai bach Rhufeinig - gynt, ceid rhes o seddau pren uwchben y draen.